The One Year Manual

The One Year Manual

formerly
Twelve Steps to Spiritual Enlightenment

Dr. Israel Regardie

SAMUEL WEISER, INC.

York Beach, Maine

This revised edition published in 1981 by
Samuel Weiser, Inc.
Box 612
York Beach, ME 03910

Third printing, 1992

Originally published under the title, *Twelve Steps to Spiritual Enlightenment*, in 1969 by the Sangreal Foundation.

First Samuel Weiser paperback edition, 1976

Library of Congress Cataloging-in-Publication Data

Regardie, Israel.
    The one year manual / by Israel Regardie.
       p.   cm.
    Includes bibliographical references.
    1. Spiritual exercises. 2. Magic I. Title.
BF1621.R43   1993
291.4'4--dc20   92-35344
                                     CIP

ISBN 0-87728-489-X
BJ

Cover painting is entitled, *The Ascent*, copyright © 1990 Rob Schouten.

Printed in the United States of America

The paper used in this publication meets the minimum requirements of the American National Standard for Permanence of Paper for Printed Library Materials Z39.48-1984.

Contents

Gratefully dedicated to
CARR P. COLLINS, JR.
who suggested and inspired this book,
and without whom it would never have been written —
or completed!

PREFACE

THIS BOOK WAS FORMERLY
entitled *Twelve Steps to Spiritual Enlightment.* Insofar as it
was intended to be a manual delineating a course of practical
study to extend over a period of at least twelve months, that
title seems rather presumptuous. It had been my original intention to entitle it *The One Year Manual.* The title describes
the nature of the book without any pretensions, assumptions
or exaggerated claims.

Several experiences wrankled in my mind not only about
the title but by the Christian references which were really quite
foreign to my outlook. The first blow came when a psychologist living in Florida corresponded with me about a couple of
my other books. Then she chanced upon the *Twelve Steps to
Spiritual Enlightenment.* It so annoyed her that she wrote me
most emphatically about her disapproval. There was nothing I
could do honestly but to write back agreeing with her and ad-
mitting that I had no great liking for these Christian references
either.

Sometime after that there was an editorial in a small
British magazine *Agape* with whose editor there had been oc-
casional correspondence. This editorial was most critical of
both me and the book. It made me realize the enormity of my
error and how far I had strayed from what was really accep-
table to me.

There were several others that hammered home the
point.

The error consisted simply of being too susceptible to the suggestions of well-meaning friends. It was their contention that the inclusion of Thelemic, Egyptian and other pagan allusions, might prove difficult to accept by some readers. Today it bothers me somewhat to admit that I was swayed by this specious argument. It was also suggested that if Christian items were to replace those mentioned above it would insure a wider circulation and sale of this book.

The outcome of all this is the revision of the book in the form originally intended before close and dear friends suggested modifications of one kind or another. Most of the material is identical with that in *Twelve Steps*. The slant, however, is totally different and may appeal to a different group of students. In its present form it adheres more closely to my original intention, and so is more to my own liking.

As previously stated, this manual delineates a course of practical study to extend over a period of at least twelve months. Theoretically, it is designed for the ideal student. Since, however, there is no such "ideal", each student represents a different problem. Each is a unique personality with his own character-structure, his own idiosyncracies and his own way of solving problems in a certain amount of time. No two students are alike.

Under these circumstances, it must be self-evident that though designed for a twelve month period, it is more likely that the student may need to spend a good five years working with these simple methods. Some exercises may be completed and mastered in the month prescribed. Other procedures may require anywhere from three months to a year before any real mastery or noticeable result is achieved. It is important therefore to stress patience as a supreme necessity where this course of study is concerned. Some exercises have as a secondary gain the acquisition of a higher degree of patience.

These simple injunctions require little elaboration. *Make haste slowly* would be the ideal maxim for every student to adopt when starting to study and practice this scheme. It will pay optimal dividends in the end.

It would be of infinite value if, while working these exercises, the student kept what I propose to call a Day Book. In accounting procedures, the Day Book is a journal in which are entered all the transactions of the day, regardless of what they are. In this Day Book, or Work Book, that we are considering, the student should keep a detailed record of every practice that he engages in. Immediately after performing every exercise, he should take a couple of minutes from his next task in order to make entries in this Day Book. He should record the date and time of the day, the particular exercise he practiced, how many minutes were devoted to it, what he felt about the manner in which he proceeded, any experiences that may have occurred, and finally his evaluation of the period itself. It might even be worthwhile recording some extraneous data, such as the kind of weather prevailing, the temperature within the room in which he is working and the general emotional mood, etc.

If this Day Book is scrupulously kept, at the expiration of a year, regardless of whether it is seen or examined by any other person, the student will eventually be able to look at his efforts with fair objectivity. It may come as a distinct surprise to read through some of his early comments on his first experiences and efforts. He may even perceive a psychological pattern running through all his exercises and whatever results accrue from them. No little insight can be obtained from this. The keeping of the Day Book, therefore, is a matter of prime importance. Meticulous attention should be given to it right from the start.

The occult student, at the outset of his studies, is besieged by hundreds of books describing dozens of practices of every kind. They promise, directly or otherwise, to bring him to the very heights of spiritual attainment, no matter how that attainment is defined. But by the very wealth of material is he overwhelmed. And the result is that, generally speaking, he does nothing except read. Reading does very little to bring one to any kind of realization of one's divine nature.

In this manual, it is proposed to burden the student with

very little theory, but to outline a course of procedure which, persisted in for at least twelve months, will bring him a good way along the Path. This course of procedure will describe a certain number of classical practices which are calculated to produce certain types of results. There will be no attempt to dazzle him with startling but vague promises, with fantasies of great achievements, with misleading claims leading nowhere.

I will simply suggest that this practice or the other, when faithfully performed, should yield such and such result. The speed with which such results are achieved naturally must vary with each student. Each human being is different, though constructed more or less on the same anatomical, physiological, psychological and spiritual basis. But within these areas there is room for a variety of differences. Such differences will determine whether he can work quickly, concentratedly, dynamically, slowly, methodically, imaginatively, or without any real vision of where he is going. But if this program is followed, he is certain at the end of a year to find himself a changed person, with a vastly changed outlook upon life, an improved perception of himself, and capable of undergoing some kind of inner discipline which ultimately will take him along the trail where former spiritual giants have trod.

It may be that when that time comes he may find himself better able to appreciate the more complex systems of training described in two occult encyclopedias which I have edited. The first, and older one, is *The Golden Dawn* (Llewellyn Publications). A profound and most effective training system is there described at great length. With his newly-found sensitivity and discipline, the student may discover this is no longer so mysterious or overwhelming as it may once have appeared. The more recent encyclopedia is *Gems from the Equinox*. This consists of the magical instructions beautifully written by Aleister Crowley for his own occult Order, the A.A. I have known many students throughout the years who, having read these instructions, have for one or more reasons been put off, finding them entirely too complicated or difficult or unintelligible. It is my belief that having completed the course of training described in this one year manual, the student may find himself far more prepared to embrace the disciplines that Crowley had recommended. In fact, I rather fancy that the Probationer of Crowley's A.A. could find this manual of the utmost value to prepare him for advancement to the Grade of Neophyte. Neither of these two Grades should pose any great problem or insuperable difficulty to the student who has first mastered the more simple disciplines outlined here.

Israel Regardie

The One Year Manual

THE FOUR ADORATIONS

IN FORMER GREAT AGES, MAN realized intuitively his relationship to nature and to the living universe in which he lived and was a part. He felt his unity with all the elements. In the fullness of his life he worshipped the Sun as a visible symbol of the unknown God *in whom we live and move and have our being.* It is axiomatic that light is life and both are dependent upon the Sun—which thus becomes a vital symbol of God.

In our modern *scientific* age of gadgets and things, with our unnatural way of life divorced from contact with the dynamic root of things, we have lost this essential wisdom. In order that we may once more progress towards the full awareness of the source of life and love and liberty, we make ritual gestures of affirming a link between the Sun and ourselves. Upon the basis of these gestures of adoration, every act in life may be dedicated in such a way that living itself becomes sanctified and transformed.

Though God is a unity, the Sun, as a symbol of God, appears differently at each of its four daily stations—dawn, noon, sunset and midnight. Therefore an adoration is directed towards the Sun at each of these four stations.

At dawn, or upon arising, he should perform whatever ablutions are customary and then turning towards the East, say audibly:

> *Hail unto Thee who art Ra in Thy rising,*
> *Even unto Thee who art Ra in Thy strength,*

> *Who travellest over the Heavens in Thy bark*
> *At the Uprising of the Sun.*
> *Tahuti standeth in His splendour at the prow*
> *And Ra-Hoor abideth at the helm.*
> *Hail unto Thee from the Abodes of Night!*

Much of the symbolism inherent in this act of simple adoration may be missed by the student for some considerable time. It does not matter just yet. But this should not be permitted to serve as an obstacle to daily practice, nor to deter him from adoring God in the form of the rising Sun every day of his life.

At noon, wherever he may be — at home, in the office, on the streets, or in a factory — let him adore God. It will help in some measure to bring God into his life. Face the South and say:

> *Hail unto Thee who art Hathor in Thy triumphing,*
> *Even unto Thee who art Hathor in Thy beauty,*
> *Who travellest over the Heavens in Thy bark*
> *At the Mid-course of the Sun.*
> *Tahuti standeth in His splendour at the prow,*
> *And Ra-Hoor abideth at the helm.*
> *Hail unto Thee from the Abodes of Morning!*

At the eventide, when the Sun goes down, let him face the West and adore the Lord of the Universe in these words:

> *Hail unto Thee, who art Tum in Thy setting,*
> *Even unto Thee who art Tum in Thy joy,*
> *Who travellest over the Heavens in Thy bark*
> *At the Down-going of the Sun.*
> *Tahuti standeth in His splendour at the prow*
> *And Ra-Hoor abideth at the helm.*
> *Hail unto Thee from the Abodes of Day!*

At midnight or upon retiring, turn to the North and say:

> *Hail unto Thee Who art Khephra in Thy hiding,*
> *Even unto Thee who art Khephra in Thy silence,*
> *Who travellest over the Heavens in Thy bark*

At the Midnight Hour of the Sun.
Tahuti standeth in his Splendour at the prow
And Ra-Hoor abideth at the helm.
Hail unto Thee from the Abodes of Evening.

This particular practice should be made a regular part of everyday life and should be persisted in until it becomes a part of your way of life. Other exercises described here may be performed for limited or varying periods of time, but these particular *Fourfold Adorations* are to be integrated for all time into the daily pattern of living.

STEP I
BODY AWARENESS

ONE OF THE MAJOR GOALS of any system of self-development or spiritual growth is the acquisition of sensitivity or self-awareness. There is only one way of acquiring this awareness — and this is to become aware.

Sitting comfortably in a straight-backed chair, or lying flat on one's back in bed, one merely attempts to observe what is happening, as it were, "under the skin." You simply watch your body, its sensations and feeling here and now. This only — and nothing more. Do not try to relax or to breathe in any unusual or special way, or to try to control the thoughts that float through the mind. All these processes and methods will be dealt with later. For the time being, merely become conscious of any sensation that arises anywhere in the body.

I suggest you wriggle around for a moment or two to find that one position which seems most comfortable. Having found it, stay in it, and do not move from it in any way. There should be absolutely no voluntary muscular movement for the rest of the practice session. Not even a wriggle of a toe, or a wiggle of a finger. The session should last not more than ten minutes at first, but gradually by the end of a month should be extended to half an hour. For many people this will seem an eternity in which every instinct will cry aloud for a wiggle of some kind to ease the tension. This should be resisted. Other students will find the ten minutes to pass, as it were, in a flash.

It is important to develop your powers of concentration while practicing these awareness exercises. If your mind wanders, gently bring it back. Your power of concentration will improve each day.

As you sit or lie quietly, you may become conscious of an itching of the scalp. Leave it alone. Do not do anything about it. Do not scratch. Just watch. In a moment or two, it may die down and disappear, or else your attention will be distracted by a tingling somewhere else. Presently, you may become conscious of the back settling down into the bed or chair. Just watch this process. Try only to become exquisitely aware of the accompanying body sensations without in the least trying to ignore them or change them.

Make no judgements about what you observe. Merely notice. Do not criticize nor reject any of these sensations. They may be comfortable or uncomfortable, pleasurable or otherwise, but they are your own. Accept them just as they are. They are you!

Sensations in different portions of the body will come and go, without apparent rhyme or reason. Watch them. It is often a good idea to verbalize audibly just what you do feel. It is a procedure I often use in my office, where I encourage the patient, lying on the couch, to express audibly enough for me to hear his description of exactly what he is presently feeling, and where.

The outcome of this is that a profound relaxation of nervous tension develops merely on the basis of watching. You do nothing else but observe the rise and fall of sensation without attempting in the least to modify whatever phenomena may occur. But day in and day out practice will heighten enormously this function that is called self–recollection, mindfulness, self-awareness, and many other names. Without this self-awareness, very little can be accomplished on the Path. All other exercises and complex procedures actually begin from this heightening of self-awareness.

Start it now. No special time need be set apart for this exercise. You may pursue it wherever you happen to be, at any time, in any place. Certainly, in bed when retiring at night, or when arising in the morning; these are excellent periods of time to practice this art of self-recollection.

While performing one's daily ablutions — bathing, washing, shaving, evacuating, applying makeup, dressing, etc. — one can sharpen one's perception of what one is doing to become conscious of the most minute and hitherto insignificant sensations.

This art can be extended enormously in a variety of different directions as familiarity with practice makes one aware of more of what is going on inside. For example, if Carl Jung's definition of psycho-therapy is that thereby one becomes conscious of what hitherto was unconscious, then the pursuit of this method will result in the heightened consciousness of a large number of inner sensations of which previously one was totally unaware. And to this extent, one's horizons of one's self will have become enlarged. The Path has been entered upon.

This exercise should be pursued for at least one month. Two practice periods should be set aside at the very least every day, no longer than ten minutes at a time. This altogether apart from the momentary cessation of activity at varying times during the day in which to observe what is going on inside.

Step II
RELAXATION

THERE ARE WELL-DEFINED techniques for developing the process of relaxation, and we can use the gains derived from the preceding exercises. Whatever position has been employed previously should be continued now. Either a supine or upright position may be used. If the latter, a stiff-backed chair to support the erect spine is undoubtedly best. If lying down on a couch or bed, the mattress should be moderately firm: but if not, the best alternative is a well-carpeted floor. The reason for this latter recommendation is that the floor will not yield, so it will have to be the practising student whose body yields to relaxation.

Before lying or sitting down, there are a couple of movements that I recommend to patients in the office. First of all, spend a minute or two, skipping with an invisible rope in a stationary position. This is not merely an exercise to enhance the blood circulation and stimulate deeper breathing, but by virtue of the alternate contraction and relaxation of muscles, it will go far towards providing the right somatic basis on which to proceed with these psychological relaxation techniques.

Following this, stand upright, with legs about a foot apart, and having inhaled, expel all the air as you let yourself fall forward from the waist, limp like a rag doll. It is similar to a calisthenic exercise of trying to touch the toes without bending the knees, falling forward completely relaxed. We are striving to produce relaxation however, not to do calisthenic exercises. Let the body above the waist fall down with the ex-

halation, with the fingers and hands dangling near the feet for
a second or two, then, as you inhale, slowly rise up to the standing position. Repeat this process a dozen or more times. It
will help you to get your wind back, after the skipping exercise
and also to relax many of the muscles of the torso. The head and
neck too should be permitted to drop limp as you exhale,
while letting the upper body drop from the waist. This will
relax the neck musculature.

Keep your mind attuned and focussed on your body sensations. Think only of what you are doing. Observe and concentrate on the various sensations of the body.

Now you are ready to begin the relaxation exercise prop-
er. Take a few very deep breaths and, as you exhale, heave
some very deep sighs. If the diaphragm and abdominal
muscles relax, the greater part of the musculature and other
tissues supplied by the involuntary or vegetative nervous
system, too, will loosen up with it. Lie quietly in this position
for a few seconds, observing yourself all the time. Become
familiar with the body; learn to notice what the body feeling is
like, becoming even more aware. The former exercises will
have acquainted you with this method and its sensations.

The next stage of the process actively employs the imagination to extend the boundaries of your awareness. There
is a well-known physiological law that an increased flow of
blood to any part of the body can be produced by concentrating on that part of the body. Whether it is merely becoming conscious of the blood already in the vessels there, or that
nervous impulses are conveyed to the muscular wall of the
arteries and vessels in the area contemplated, thus relaxing
those walls to permit an enhanced blood-flow, does not matter; either explanation will suffice. That this can be done is an
actual experience you can demonstrate to yourself.

By knowing that there are tensions in a certain limb or
organ we can, by using the imagination, stimulate vasodilator
fibers which relax blood-vessels enabling the blood to flow
there in larger quantities. A surplus of blood—a congestion—will cause a degree of heat which in turn will induce the

relaxation of muscular fibre and tissue that we desire. This is the theory; it leads directly to practice.

It calls for the active use of the imagination. First of all, visualize your brain. Everyone has seen diagrams and drawings of the brain frequently enough to know what it looks like in the main, without naming the technical neurological details. It is a mass of white and gray substance, convoluted and twisted in upon itself, divided by a long fissure into two lateral hemispheres, with a front and rear portion. Picture it, as you have seen it in the drawings. Hold the picture firmly in your mind until you begin to sense a warm feeling spreading out from the center of the skull. Sometimes it may be accompanied by a gentle tingling, a pins-and-needles sensation. Facilitate this process by imagining that the blood-vessels within the brain have dilated enough to hold larger amounts of blood, thus turning the brain pink, and that this congestion has produced the warmth that has already been sensed.

From the brain proceed to the eyes, imagining that these are like two balls, each hanging from four tiny muscular chains. Manage this picture as you have the previous one. By building the imaginative picture, the lumen of the blood vessels in the muscles become enlarged and hold more blood which warms the surrounding musculature. They then relax, yielding the sensation of the eyeballs sinking back into their sockets.

It is important to develop your powers of concentration while practicing these relaxation exercises. Do not allow your mind to wander from what you are doing, or more particularly, from the area you are relaxing. Concentrate. Think only on what you are doing. If your mind wanders, gently bring it back. Your power of concentration will improve each day.

Pursue a similar procedure with regard to the rest of the head—that is, visualize the warm blood flowing through widened blood-vessels to the temples, the ears, the cheekbones, then to the nose, mouth, lips, tongue, jaws and chin. In much the same way, after having made the mental constructs, you will feel warmth and tingling build up in the areas imagined, with the gradual emergence of the relaxed feeling.

By the time you have gone thus far—and at least ten minutes should have been spent in this action—the greater part of the body will reflexively have undergone a relaxing process. No matter how greatly relaxed you felt after the first exercise of merely observing your body—this merely prepared the pathway. The current exercises carry them tremendously further.

The remaining part of the half hour—and the exercise for this month should take not one minute less—should be devoted to dealing with every part of the body in much the same way as described above. The whole neck should be dealt with thoroughly. Work down easily through the shoulders and the arms until the abdominal area is reached. Give this then a thorough working over. The more you relax this middle area of the abdomen, the more likely it is that the whole of your body will respond with massive "letting-go". Dr. Georg Groddeck, the father of modern psychosomatic medicine, called this area the "middle-man" of the body. In the beautiful imagery and psychological symbolism that this physician employed, this middle part of the body was conceived to be endowed with a species of intelligence even as is the breast and the head—this *belly-mind* being often opposed to the cold inclinations and rational activities of the *head-mind*. It is the seat of the instincts, feelings and passions, and all the dynamic forces inherited from the past that we attribute to the Unconscious.

Finally, visualize the stream of blood separating from the aorta into two powerful arterial streams, two rivers of warm blood descending from the pelvis into the thighs, legs and feet. Be very attentive here, too; visualize all the tight, stiff, taut thigh and leg muscles thoroughly in order to relax them under the stimulus of the imagination and the warmth of the blood. In this manner, proceed until the toes are reached. Then pause.

You have completed a great cycle in the relaxing process.

Pause to consider and observe. Note how you feel. Your previous work should have heightened your ability to sense what is happening somatically. Record your feelings. Permit the sense of real pleasure and enjoyment and freedom to make an indelible impression upon your mind.

If the memory of this experience is well-recorded, it can be evoked at any moment from your storehouse of memories. It doesn't matter if you are riding in the subway or driving your car, at home reading or listening to the radio, you have only to remember the pleasure of relaxation and forthwith the memory is evoked from your psyche to impact itself upon all the tissues and fibres of the body. Relaxation then follows.

It is well to enjoy this feeling of deep relaxation. Impress it thoroughly upon your mind. Get the feel of complete relaxation as vividly and as strongly as you can, because henceforth, when you need to relax, you can restore this state of calmness, serenity and complete relaxation merely by thinking of it.

When you next want to relax, all you have to do is take a deep breath and as you exhale, think of the word *relax* and remember this wonderful serene feeling of complete relaxation and once again it will be immediately restored to you. Inhale and as you breathe out, mentally command yourself to relax. Soon this conditioned reflex will be immediate, automatic and complete.

Approximately half an hour at a time should be given over to this practice. If you are able to, pursue the process twice a day, morning and evening. Concentrate on the formation of the conditioned reflex which will then produce the relaxed state without the loss of valuable time. But there must be considerable practice first before the conditioned reflex can be established. Once a day will do; twice a day is better. In this way, the foundation is laid down for the more significant and spiritual work to be developed and worked upon later.

As an aside, it might be worth recording that this exercise in one form or another, is now being used in the treatment of cancer. In Texas there is a husband-wife team, physician and psychologist, the Drs. Carl Simonton who teach their patients relaxation methods which are similar to this. The patients then add their own personal flourishes to the technique. For example, one may imagine that the blood sweeping through a cancerous growth is breaking down the malignancy, to sweep it away for elimination elsewhere. Yet another may imagine a host of knights in shining armor bearing down on the malignancy and slashing it to bits. There are innumerable variations to be rung on this simple theme. As a supplement or as an addendum to orthodox medical treatment, a high percentage of "cures" is claimed which is not obtainable by using one or the other exclusively.

As a further extension of the technique described here, it would be well to note that all the current experiments with bio-feedback instruments corroborate in every detail the fundamental thesis of this chapter.

Step III
RHYTHMIC BREATHING

After the exercises on awareness and relaxation have been practiced, the attention can be turned to breathing. First of all, it can be stated dogmatically that few of us breathe adequately. The preceding exercise should have demonstrated the existence of massive tensions in the entire chest, diaphragmatic and abdominal areas of the body. These tensions hamper the breathing process. Self-awareness and relaxation will have modified these tensions if not entirely, then at least in part.

Self-observation will further have revealed that many of us breathe only with the upper portion of the lungs. For example, men who wear tight belts will find that they are forced to breathe with the higher chest area because the diaphragm and abdomen are compressed by the tight belt. On the other hand, women who wear tight brassieres may discover that the effort involved in lifting the chest against the tight compression of the elastic part of the brassiere is entirely too great, so that it is easier to use the middle or lower area of the lungs. Moreover, those with severe emotional problems will have discovered that invariably the entire breathing process is hampered by massive muscular tension, resulting in very poor oxygenation—and therefore very low vitality.

The attention given to breathing on the Path of Enlightenment has as one of its objects the eradication of as much neuromuscular tension as possible and therefore the heightening of energy and vitality. An attempt is made to regulate the process of breathing in a rhythmical manner. Its necessity arises from the following notion: if life is all one, all-penetrant and all-pervasive, what more reasonable then, that the very air we breathe from one moment to another should be highly charged with vitality? Our breathing process is then regulated on the basis that life is the active principle in the atmosphere, whether we call it oxygen, prana or something else.

During the practice of this rhythmic breathing at fixed periods of the day—twice a day at least, and for no more than ten minutes at a time—there should be no strenuous forcing of the mind, no overtaxing of the will. All effort should be gentle and easy; then skill is obtained. Let the breath flow in while mentally counting very slowly...one, two, three, four. Then exhale counting to the same fourfold beat.

It is fundamental and important that the initial rhythm begun, whether it be at a four or a ten beat count, or any other convenient rhythm, should be maintained for the ten minutes prescribed. It is the very rhythm itself which is responsible for the ready absorption of vitality from without, and the acceleration of the divine power within.

In working for the development of the rhythmic breath, the student should not reject the possibility of using mechanical devices. In the opening phases of self-applied discipline, the student needs every bit of help he can obtain. I would like to suggest the use of one of the modern electric metronomes attached to a timer as being supremely useful. The combination of these two instruments will accomplish the following:

1. Set an automatic limit to the practice session.
2. Eliminate anxiety as to the duration of the session.
3. Permit a rapid or slow beat on the metronome which one can follow in the breathing pattern.
4. It can be adjusted to produce a loud or soft click.
5. It provides an extraneous but not superfluous sound which can be concentrated on while developing the rhythmic breath.

A number of things are thus accomplished in one fell

swoop. It might also be noted that when the student approaches the development of a mantram of any kind to accompany the rhythmic breath, the metronome will be found to be most useful.

In fact, this topic of the mantram might just as as well be touched on lightly at this point. A classical Christian mantram is *Lord Jesus Christ, have mercy on me.* It does not matter whether you wish our Lord to have mercy on you or not. It does not even matter whether or not you believe in Jesus. The issue at hand is that these words can be put to a type of beat to be paced by the metronome which in turn times the rhythm of the breathing.

So, for example on the inhalation to a slow four-fold beat, the student who is sympathetic to the Christian mythos can silently intone *Lord...Jes...Us...Christ* one cycle, and on the exhalation *have...mercy...on...me* as the second cycle. Only a very little practice will be required to get the mantram going. If help is required, the student can tap the beat with his finger in time with the metronome. Or the two phrases could be dictated into a tape recorder, which can be played back over and over again, until the rhythm and mantram are mastered. This is relatively easy to acquire, and the results obtained are worth what little time and energy are expended for mastery.

In attempting to attune ourselves anew to the intelligent spiritual power operating throughout all of nature, we attempt, not blindly to copy, but rationally to adopt her methods. Make therefore the breathing rhythmical at certain fixed times of the day when there is little likelihood of disturbance.

Cultivate beyond all other things, the art of relaxation. A great deal of emphasis will be placed on this process. Practice of the preceding method of self-observation will go far towards mastering this art. When some degree of relaxation has been achieved, then you should begin your rhythmic breathing exercise, slowly and without haste. Gradually, as the mind accustoms itself to the idea, the lungs spontaneously take up the rhythm. Within a few minutes it will have become automatic. The whole process then becomes extremely simple and pleasurable.

Simple as it is, the exercise should never be despised because of being in a hurry to get to more complicated or advanced procedures. It is upon the mastery of this very easy technique that much of this one-year system depends. Master it first. Ensure your depth relaxation, and then proceed with the rhythmic breath.

It would be difficult to overestimate its importance or efficacy. As the lungs take up the rhythm, automatically inhaling and exhaling to a measured beat, so do they communicate it and gradually extend it to all the surrounding body cells and tissues. Just as a stone thrown into a pond sends out widely expanding ripples and concentric circles of motion, so does the motion of the lungs. In a few minutes, the whole body will be felt to vibrate sympathetically. Very soon, the entire organism comes to feel as if it were an inexhaustible storage battery of power. The sensation — and it must be a sensation, not a mere fantasy — is unmistakable.

A rationale for this type of breathing may be found in these theories:

First, the intaking of large quantities of oxygen has a distinct effect on the endocrines which undergo an enormous stimulation. This may be primarily due to the improved circulation of blood that follows from the rhythmic excursions of the diaphragm.

Second, in his book *Raja Yoga,* the late Swami Vivekananda provided an admirable explanation of the effect of regulated breathing, which strengthens and stimulates the Will into a most formidable concentration of power. Briefly, his theory is that by making all the cells in one's body vibrate in unison, as they do during the rhythmic breath, a powerful electric current of *will* or *spiritual energy* is instituted in the body and mind.

Third, the Will undergoes a serious training. Any individual who has attempted breathing exercises for even a few minutes will understand what is meant. Anything more tedious and laborious and wearisome at first sight than this simple exercise could hardly be imagined. It calls for the exertion of the utmost determination to continue. In doing so, the individual is brought sharply to face the inertia and lassitude he lives by, requiring no little discipline and self-conquest to persist in this appointed task. This becomes easier with mastery and the emergence of considerable body pleasure.

In any event, if the student has obtained no technical book-described result whatsoever, he will at least have gained an immeasurable increase in willpower and indomitability of purpose in having trained himself to overcome his own slothfulness. "To learn self-conquest is, therefore, to learn how to live, and the austerities of stoicism were no idle boast of liberty. To resist and overcome nature is to achieve for oneself a personal and imperishable existence; it is to set oneself free from the vicissitudes of life and death," so wrote Eliphas Levi about a century ago.

STEP IV
MIND AWARENESS

THE DIFFERENCE BETWEEN this exercise and the previous awareness exercise is that the area of attention is shifted from bodily processes to those of the mind. In psychoanalysis, this is commonly referred to as free association. One simply permits the mind to wander as it will, letting it move without hindrance in any direction where it may be attracted. The student simply watches. This, and nothing else.

It is rather like turning a horse out to pasture, without rope or saddle or blanket; there is nothing to interfere with its free movement. In this practice, one rapidly proves for oneself one of the basic theorems of psychoanalysis, that all thoughts are strictly determined. One discovers soon enough that one can trace every thought to a causative chain extending far back into the past. You may appreciate this theoretically; it remains to be discovered empirically.

"Until you know what the mind is doing you cannot control it." So said a great sage, Vivekananda, over sixty years ago. It is still true. He went on to say, "Give it the full length of the reins; many most hideous thoughts may come into it; you will be astonished that it was possible for you to think such thoughts. But you will find that each day the mind's vagaries are becoming less and less violent, that each day it is becoming calmer. In the first few months you will find that the mind will have a thousand thoughts, later you will find that it is toned down to perhaps seven hundred, and after a few more months it will have fewer and fewer, until at last it will be under perfect control, but we must patiently practice every day. As soon as the steam is turned on the engine must run, and as soon as things are before us we must perceive; so a man, to prove that he is not a machine, must demonstrate that he is under the control of nothing."

One should determine beforehand how long each session of introspection practice should be. If you decide that it shall be for half an hour, then use an alarm clock or a kitchen timer set for that period of time. Once it has sounded off, the practice should be stopped promptly. In this way, one will not be carried away over-enthusiastically by this process of observing what is going on within the mind itself.

The most comfortable and effective position for this practice is to sit in a straight chair, using a pillow at the back, head up, eyes closed, knees straight and together, hands resting easily in the lap or on the knees, and back straight. The most important thing to remember is that the body must always be perfectly balanced, erect, comfortable and relaxed. All the preceding work should have rendered this position relatively easy.

A favorite device of mine is to employ a tape recorder. It should be so prepared that it will run for a full hour without the need for the slightest bit of attention. This is not to state that the practice-session should last for an hour. On the contrary, thirty minutes is ample, at any one time. The student could practice twice, or even three times per day if he has the opportunity and inclination. As time goes on, and as proficiency is gained, then the time of practice could be extended considerably. But the recorder should be able to handle at least the half-hour recommended, and perhaps a full hour in the event you get carried away by the process.

While sitting upright and motionless in the meditative position, quietly verbalize audibly to the microphone nearby any thought, memory, idea or feeling that happens to arise within. Talk at random, without premeditation.

Usually, the results are illuminating—as well as shocking.

It will give the student an idea of what "stuff" lies concealed within his psyche. They are sometimes shocking only if one has been wholly honest in expressing the inner content of the mind as it arises. The development of some mental honesty is a tremendous gain.

Once one has really become aware of the hidden content of consciousness, and has struggled to come to terms with oneself, the inner conflicts produced by the censorship of the superego or conscience are considerably reduced. So also will be the number of "breaks" in concentration produced by pressure of these repressed ideational and emotional contents within the psyche.

The practice of introspection or "uncontrolled" free association recording and playback should be pursued for some length of time, until the shock and dismay usually experienced upon the realization of the hideous thinking one is capable of, has been dissipated or reduced to practically zero. Then one is ready to attack the process of concentration directly.

What is important beyond all other things is that in the process of watching and observing the random flow of thoughts and feelings there should be no judgment or criticism or self-condemnation. "Judge not lest ye be judged!" Once the initial shock has worn off, it is more than likely that the student will take the same bemused attitudes towards the mental contents, as it were, as he did towards his physical sensations when merely observing his body. To criticize or condemn oneself is foolish, even infantile. Your thoughts have to be accepted as part of your total equipment, untrained, unskilled and undisciplined. With training and application, these infantile elements within the psyche can be turned in other directions and their latent energy employed for nobler and higher ends.

The student must also be reminded of the tentative nature of the attributions of exercises to months. The slower student, and most of us come within this category, should allow several months at the very least to deal adequately with this topic of introspection. The more advanced student, who has been exposed to similar types of training before, may very likely sail through this set of exercises like a breeze. These people, however, are few and far between. Most should realize that it is going to take time to achieve skill and mastery in these methods.

It should be remembered that where there is haste, there is waste. I still like the old maxim — *solvitur ambulando.* Solve your problems as you proceed. Feel that you do not have to rush to prove that you are bright or very spiritual.

STEP V
CONCENTRATION:
USE OF THE MANTRAM

BY NOW, THE STUDENT SHOULD be considerably familiar with his own sensations, feelings and thoughts. The practices heretofore laid down should have created a high degree of sensitivity to these phases of himself so that with the beginning of concentration exercises he will be under no delusion as to what exists in the kingdom within. Once he begins to practice concentration and meditation, it will be as though all the forces within himself arise in open revolt against this discipline. Ancient memories and infantile feelings will become activated by the exercise and may disturb him unless he has achieved a high degree of self-awareness. It is in the acquisition of this awareness that much of the value of the former exercises exist.

The previous exercises should have resulted in the acquisition of some degree of peace and quiet. A sense of well-being and inner assurance will arise from within. It is in the tranquillity and calmness now developed that permits, as it were, the mind to open up and receive the influx of the Holy Spirit. But practice is the first and last essential.

It should be easier to set up more frequent and short periods of mental work during the day so as to train the mind more effectively to concentrate. These periods of quiet, inner observation and reflection, introspection and concentration, will prepare the student to receive the inner Light. Even though at first no progress *seems* to be made, and no response is felt, discouragement must not be permitted to occur to dampen one's ardor nor to bring about a cessation of effort. The student has no way at the moment of gauging his progress. Immediate results are not, as a rule, forthcoming. With serious intent, the whole concept of expecting something to happen quickly will be given up, with the emphasis being placed on the advantages of teaching the mind an important and highly necessary discipline.

In the process of acquiring this faculty of concentration, there will be a number of side-effects which are of the utmost importance. The first is the development of the Will, and secondly, the Imagination or image-building faculty will undergo a vast improvement. Both of these faculties will prove to be infinitely valuable in the process of inner growth and development. Some of the results from the later exercises will hinge on the use of these inner faculties, the king faculties, socalled, of Will and Imagination.

The student will have already discovered what a menagerie he has inside him. The attempts to observe the body sensations at the beginning of this work, followed by watching the flow of thoughts and ideas without interfering with their movement, will have shown him something of the nature of his inner world. These cannot be ignored nor can they be fought and suppressed. The mere attempt to do this will heighten their intrusion and give them power which ordinarily they do not have. But as they are observed and watched, they tend to diminish in frequency and potency, and thus create the right conditions for the development of concentration.

It is this achievement which sets the stage for the beginning of work on concentration and later, meditation. In order to achieve this power, some preliminaries are useful. It is well to remember that though our ultimate goal is to achieve an inner state of calm and quiet, we should never try to *force* the mind into quiescence, never try to stop thinking or to deliberately blank out our thoughts. It is an impossible goal anyway. We have to learn patience to conquer any sense of restlessness. In order to acquire this patience, there are methods to be used which will facilitate our progress to this ultimate end.

The mind is a creature of habits. No less an authority than William James has averred that old worthless habits can be broken only in the development of new constructive ones. The mind has a natural tendency to adopt habits. You know how we get into the habit of doing things, particularly habits of doing things at a definite time of day. Thus we get into the habit of waking up at a definite time of the morning, eating breakfast and lunch and dinner at certain times, not because we are really hungry but because we have developed the habit of eating at those hours. Once the pattern is set, we usually tend to wake up or to go to bed at the same hours. In effect, the practice of any act, the persistence of any given set of ideas, regularly occurring at a set time of the day, results in a very powerful tendency to the recurrence of those ideas, or to the practice of that act at the same time every day.

It is this fact that we use to assist us in our practice of concentration. Choose a given time of day. Always practice at that same time, even if it is only for ten minutes, but always at exactly the same time of the day, in the same room, and in the same chair or posture. In a little while, the habit will have become established like a conditioned reflex and you will find it much easier to concentrate the mind at this time than at any other. In fact, if you try to skip practice at that hour, you are likely to experience a sense of dis-ease or of anxiety, which will then force you to get down to work.

If you have a specific room that could be reserved solely for your practices, so much the better. The burning of a stick of incense or lighting a candle may assist in the eliciting of a devotional mood which may dispose to hard work. However, if there is no extra room and if incense cannot be burned or a candle lighted, do not despair or regard these as obstacles or consider yourself doomed. They are merely conveniences and nothing more.

Another simple traditional device for slowing down the rapid movement of the mind is known as a mantram. Apart from more technical considerations, a mantram is simply a word or a phrase, usually of a religious nature, which is repeated over and over again, either audibly or subvocally, until it is taken up by the mind itself. In that case, the phrase goes on repeating itself automatically. Thus a mechanical aid to concentration is perfected, which can then be used to further the predetermined goals.

For those with a predilection for Christian prayer and symbolism, the previously described method should prove ideal. To others, whose hearts may be elsewhere, let me suggest the following Hindu mantram. It too, has eight syllables, which can be broken down into two lines of four beats each:

> *Om Na Ma Ha*
> *Shi Va Ya Om*

This invocation should be memorized, which is easy, and then recited mentally in time with the breathing. On the inhalation say: *Om Na Ma Ha* and on the exhalation: *Shi Va Ya Om*. With only a little effort, the mantram becomes relatively easy to recite, timed by the breathing process.

Once it has become relatively automatic, the student can reflect more on what the phrases mean, and with what passion they are or can be endowed. It is this emotional force which directs the mind one-pointedly towards the maintenance of the mantram until concentration is an everpresent fact. The loading of emotion onto the mechanical repetition of the prayer forces the recalcitrant mind to behave, inducing a deep state of concentration. With some practice, the concentration can be turned on and off until it becomes a faculty which is as readily available as is the electric current in the modern home.

Again, it must be repeated, that although theoretically a month is allocated to this particular exercise, it may be necessary to extend considerably the period of time required to obtain familiarity with and mastery over the method. If it requires six months, then by all means continue to work patiently on the mantram, because the goals you have in mind are not limited merely to a six-month period. They are going to operate through and alter the whole course of your future life. So there is no point talking about one month or twelve months, or of hastening the process. All that is important is to keep one's nose patiently to the grindstone of the holy labor which at this stage is the acquisition of concentration.

STEP VI
DEVELOPING THE WILL

In his introduction to *The Yoga Sutras of Patanjali,* William Q. Judge makes the statement that the ancient Hindu sages knew the secret of the development of the Will, and how to increase both its potency and efficacy. This secret of the ages, the enhancement of the power of Will and Wisdom, has never really been lost. Will, to the student of the Mysteries, is the primary factor in the production of whatever spiritual changes he proposes. It is neither good nor bad in itself; it is power only, and vitalizes all things alike.

The secret of the development of the Will is to set up certain goals and if deflected from observing them, to deprive oneself of something that gives one pleasure. Let it be clearly understood here that there is nothing good nor bad in this process. To deprive oneself of, let us say, breakfast as a punishment for having missed the morning practice, does not make one virtuous or good, nor should it result in the feeling that having given up several hundred calories of nutrition there is a moral gain in a metabolic loss of weight. It must be realized at the start that this method, which we can call a species of modified asceticism, is neither a vice nor virtue, neither good nor bad, just as Will itself is colorless and is neither good nor bad in itself.

A variety of techniques have been erected on this basic proposition and some extremely efficient methods have been evolved in recent years — methods free from all the unpleasant implications and moral tendencies of the older systems.

Perhaps the most effective method of reinforcement of the

conditioned response is to administer a mild electric shock. In most magic or trick store you will be able to find a small gadget which will administer a very light shock when the insert is pulled from the surrounding container. The shock is slight, but the surprise value is considerable. If this is used immediately following the broken vow or forbidden action, the association will become fixed and a constant vigilance on the part of the Will is set up. For this reason it is necessary that you carry the gadget with you at all times so that the shock can be given immediately after a violation has occurred. In this way, forbidden action and the electric shock will be conjoined.

According to this system, the technique is so arranged as to include the entire field of human action, speech and thought, and thus is applicable to the entire constitution of man. It is in agreement with the general concept of discipline that a certain action, word or thought which has become habitual and involuntary, should be denied or negated. Such as for example, vowing for a provisional period of time, say a week, to refrain from crossing the legs over the knee when sitting down, or perhaps not to raise the left hand to head or face. The great advantage is that there is no moral bias in these suggestions. It is not virtuous to refrain from crossing the knees or not touching the face with the left hand. Thus the student is delivered from the tendency of making a foolish virtue of his discipline.

It is necessary also to observe that there is no suggestion to apply the ascetic principle in this scheme to what is commonly termed a bad habit, such as smoking, drinking or swearing. To do so would be to invite certain individuals with compulsive neuroses to regard their abstinence as a virtue to be highly commended, instead of realizing that the denial is simply a matter of convenience and training, a personal idiosyncrasy to which neither credit nor blame should be attached. A thoroughly impersonal attitude of detachment should be maintained. The application of the scheme is necessary to those actions, words and thoughts to which it is altogether impossible to attribute a moral worth. It is not conceivable that the intelligent student will make a religious virtue of the fact that he refrains from crossing his knees or that on occasion he does not touch his head with his left hand. He can formulate other tasks for this purpose.

Now for every violation of this vow to refrain from a certain course of action, a certain punishment should be inflicted. It is in this discipline that the Will derives its training and its strength. For instance, assume the student to have decided to refrain for a period of forty-eight hours from crossing the right knee over his left leg when seated. During a moment of forgetfulness, and there will be many, it may be that the student performs the proscribed deed. That violation should be immediately punished, so as to make a lasting impression on the mind either by an act or by depriving oneself of something that ordinarily gives pleasure.

One could go without breakfast or a dessert after dinner, or should one smoke, eliminating the mid-morning cigarette or pipe. I think the electric shocker is better. The forbidden action thus becomes associated with pain or a deprivation of pleasure and soon becomes reinforced by repetition into a conditioned reflex. This will shortly operate automatically without the student having to give the matter any conscious attention. A curious vigilance on the part of the Will is set up, a free unconscious flow of attention being ever present and ready to execute the wishes of the student. One will soon discover that when chatting in casual conversation and in a state of utter forgetfulness of the vow, any automatic tendency of the legs, for example, to repeat thoughtlessly the habit to which they have long become accustomed, will immediately be detected by the Will long before the proscribed act is even half-way completed and the tendency will be stopped in its inception.

The consequence is obvious. As time progresses, the student accomplishes two separate things, both of them being major aspects of the Great Work. A perpetual vigilance approximating a very powerful current of Will-power has been generated. This, from the beginning, tends to bring the multifarious activities of the human psyche under conscious control of the Will.

An even more important result, from our present point of view, is that not only does the student find himself in possession of a stronger Will, but that the mind itself has gradually placed itself under control. The loss of pleasure is experienced almost as if pain were inflicted, and we all shrink from its repetition. So rather than experience pain or displeasure, a control is exerted which results in an easier control of the mind, facilitating the development of concentration.

As an aside, it might be mentioned that the method described has its modern counterpart in what is called behavior modification or aversion therapy. Essentially it is predicated on the original work of Pavlov, decades ago, with the conditioned reflex. It has been used with considerable success even in such prosaic matters as weight control and the eradication of the smoking habit. Modifications initiated by the psychologist Skinner have a wide current usage reaching even into various aspects of our penal institutions and prisoner rehabilitation.

STEP VII
THE ROSE CROSS RITUAL

A NEW TYPE OF WORK WILL BE introduced in order to avoid the possibility of boredom or of slipping into the dull rut of routine. Most of the previous work has been subjective. Now in the present work, the student will make his first tentative exploration into the simplest form of ritual where both subjective and physical activities become combined.

I suggest that the student obtain some sticks of incense. It doesn't really matter what kind or what fragrance they give off. He could visit any one of the local oriental or psychedelic stores and savor a variety of the incense sticks, finally selecting one that pleases him the most.

The next thing is to practice with a stick of incense, making a form of the cross with a circle inside. The imagination must be used when tracing this cross that we can call the Rose Cross. Hold out the incense stick in the right hand at above the level of the eyes and trace a straight line down, stopping somewhere opposite the knees. While tracing this vertical line, visualize it in pale blue—not too dissimilar to the color produced when burning alcohol. Then bring the arm and the stick to a level opposite the left shoulder, moving over to the right shoulder. This too should be visualized in the pale blue as clearly as possible. Disengage the incense stick from the cross bar and point it at the vertical bar, about half way between the cross bar and the beginning point of the vertical bar. From this point trace a circle moving to the right and downwards and then up and left to complete the circle. This completes the Rose Cross. It should appear to the imagination something like this:

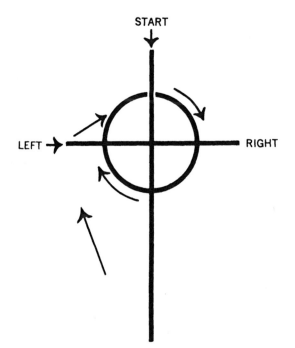

Two sacred names should be pronounced or vibrated in the process of tracing this figure. Both are of Qabalistic origin, dating from the Middle Ages. While both are variants of the name of Jesus in the Hebrew tongue, the exact meaning and the symbolism of the name are of no concern to us at this present moment. The names are: YEHESHUAH and YEHOVASHAH. The first name should be vibrated while tracing the cross — that is, both the upright and cross bars, and the second name should be voiced during the formation of the circle. Practice making the cross in the above-described manner and vibrating the two names until there is not a moment's doubt as to what you are doing. When skill has been achieved, then you can proceed to the full ritual.

Face the East. Place the lighted incense on the altar or table in front of you. Raise and extend your arms out from your sides, thereby forming a cross.

    1. Intone the following invocation.

I am He! The Bornless Spirit! Having sight in the Feet!
Strong and the Immortal Fire!
I am He! The Truth!
I am He! Who hate that evil should be wrought in the World!
I am He that lighteneth and thundereth.
I am He from Whom the Shower of the Life of Earth:
I am He, Whose mouth ever flameth:
I am He, the Begetter and Manifester unto the Light.
I am He, the Grace of the World!
'The Heart Girt With a Serpent' is my Name!
Come thou forth and follow me, and make all spirits subject unto me: so that every spirit of the Firmament and of the Ether upon the Earth and under the Earth; on dry land and in the Water, of Whirling Air and of rushing Fire and every Spell and Scourge of God, the Vast One, shall be obedient unto me.

Return arms to your side. Pause and reflect upon the meaning intrinsic to the invocation.

    2. Extend the right arm in front of you and with the lighted incense stick, trace the first Rose Cross in the East. Vibrate softly but powerfully the two sacred names.

    3. Pointing the incense stick to the center of the Cross, move towards the right, and facing the South, trace another Rose Cross, vibrating the same names.

    4. Pointing the incense stick to the center of the Cross, move towards the right, and facing the West, trace another Rose Cross, vibrating the same names.

    5. Pointing the incense stick to the center of the Cross, move towards the right and facing the North, trace another Rose Cross, vibrating the same Names.

    6. Pointing the incense stick to the center of the Cross, move towards the right, thus returning to the East, and thrust

the incense stick to the center of the previously traced Rose Cross of the East, therewith completing the circle.

7. From this point, raise the arm and incense stick towards the ceiling, moving towards the West, but stopping halfway between East and West. Trace towards the ceiling another Rose Cross, vibrating the same two names.

8. Proceed to the West, touching imaginatively the center of the Rose Cross previously made. Then lowering the arm and incense stick, move back towards the East, but stopping in the center. pointing towards the floor, trace another Rose Cross and vibrate the same two names.

9. Proceed towards the East, touching imaginatively the center of the Rose Cross previously made.

10. From here, proceed to the right, to the South. Raise the arm and incense stick towards the ceiling, moving towards the North, but stopping halfway between South and North. Trace towards the ceiling another Rose Cross, vibrating the same two Names.

11. Proceed to the North, touching imaginatively the center of the Rose Cross previously made. Then lowering the arm and incense stick, move back towards the South, but stopping in the center. Pointing towards the floor, trace another Rose Cross and vibrate the two names.

12. Proceed towards the South, touching imaginatively the center of the Rose Cross previously made.

13. These gestures will have resulted in the tracing of the Rose Cross symbol all around you, in every cardinal quarter, above and below you. From the South, extend the arm and incense stick and walk, moving to the right, back to the East, completing the circle of the place.

14. Then proceed with the second part of the invocation, extending the arms in the form of a cross:

*Unto Thee Sole Wise, Sole Mighty and Sole Eternal One,
    be Praise and Glory forever,
Who has permitted me to enter thus far into the
    Sanctuary of Thy Mysteries,
Not unto me, but unto Thy name be the Glory.*

Let the influence of Thy Divine Ones descend upon my head and teach me the value of self-sacrifice so that I shrink not in the hour of trial. But that thus my name may be written on high and my Genius stand in the presence of the Holy One, in that hour when the Son of Man is invoked before the Lord of Spirits and His Name in the presence of the Ancient of Days.

15. Lower the arms, and sit down quietly in a chair in the center of the circle. Achieve relaxation and rhythmic breathing by the use of the command for the conditioned reflex. Once relaxation has occurred, meditate upon the meaning of the ritual and of the opening and closing invocations.

This Ritual should be performed twice a day for the current month. It should never be done hastily or perfunctorily, but slowly, solemnly and reverently. The student should allow at least half an hour for the performance of the ritual and followed by its related meditation.

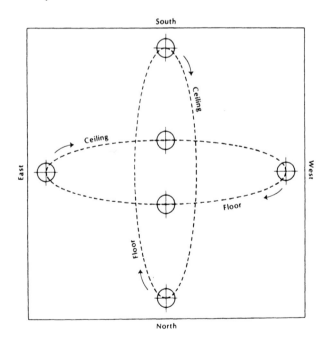

Rose Cross Ritual

Step VIII
THE MIDDLE PILLAR RITUAL

IN THIS REGIMEN OF SPIRITUAL discipline, every attempt has been made to avoid reference to foreign systems or the use of strange words or names with which the average student might not be familiar. In this exercise we want to use some Hebrew words or divine names. There is no virtue *per se* in these words. They are traditional and they emit a type of sound vibration which is useful to us — and that is all. No other English words have been found which quite serve the same purpose. The student must therefore understand that no religious prejudice is involved in the utilization of these words.

The method to be described is called the Middle Pillar Ritual — though it is not a formalized ritual in the accepted sense of the term. It is derived from an archaic mystical philosophy called the Qabalah. The central schema of this philosophy is known as the Tree of Life, which consists of ten centers arranged in a pattern of Three Pillars. We are concerned here solely with the Middle Pillar, the Pillar of *Balance* situated between the other two columns of *Severity* and *Mercy*.

Let the student be seated in his now habitual meditation position. Start off with rhythmic breathing which should be persisted in for a few minutes until the ripple in the solar plexus is initiated, by which time the rhythm should be automatic.

Some authorities have asserted that the higher spiritual Self is not fully incarnated in the average human being, but only overshadows him. Much of the intent of this excercise is to heighten awareness of this divine overshadowing and to permit a more complete permeation of the mind-body system by the higher self or Holy Guardian Angel as it has archaically been called.

To facilitate the development of the requisite mood, the student might initiate the entire Ritual with a prayer such as:

Holy art thou Lord of the Universe for thy glory flows out to the ends of the Universe, rejoicing.
Be with me now in this, the Great Work,
which I dedicate wholly to Thee.
Be my mind open to the Higher.
Be my heart a center of the Light.
Be my body a temple of the Holy Spirit.

Later, when maximum force and energy is to be generated, it is recommended that the prayer or invocation be followed with the Bornless Spirit invocation of the previous chapter for additional reinforcement and exaltation.

Visualize a bright light just over the head in the form of a sphere or ball about the diameter of a saucer or salad plate. Concentrate upon its scintillating brilliance, imagining it whirling and vibrating, and very soon there will be some awareness, some sensation-feeling of something being activated above the head. When this is felt, vibrate the word EHEIEH — pronounced E h-huh-yeh. (Again, let me insist, the meaning of these words is of little import here; only their sound value is of use to us now.) These syllables are equally emphasized and should be vibrated slowly, getting the maximum sound out of each syllable. With a little practice, the word can be so vibrated as to appear to be wholly concentrated in that sphere of light above the head. If there is any tendency for the mind to wander — though once the sensations are felt, the mind concentrates almost automatically as though fascinated — repeat the vibration of the name. Vibrate the name several times; there is no set limit. The vibration need not be loud, a vigorous humming is really all that is required. As time goes on, the whole procedure can be performed mentally, with the vibration being performed sub-vocally, that is, silently. But only after the technique has been mastered orally — not until then.

In the event that some difficulty is experienced in feeling where this center is, a little ancillary aid is useful. Obtain from the local drugstore a proprietary medicine named HEET. The cork comes equipped with a little dauber. Find the spot on top of the head from which the hair radiates, and apply a tiny dab of this HEET. Rub it in very gently with the fingers until you can *feel* where the irritant is, for in reality, this product is merely an irritant to stimulate the blood circulation to that area. Then pause for a moment and repeat the above directions — that there is a ball of whirling light above the head.

After you have concentrated on this sphere of light above the head for approximately five minutes, or until it feels sufficiently activated, then imagine a shaft of light issuing from it, going down through the head to the throat and neck. Here it expands to form another sphere of light that extends from the front to the back of the neck. Formulate this sphere as vividly as you can, using the divine name YHVH ELOHIM. This is pronounced YUH-Hoh-voh Eh-loh-heem, no one syllable being more strongly accented than the other. Vibrate the name several times, focusing it within this second sphere, using a similar procedure as before, until there is a clear vivid awareness of this second sphere vibrating in the neck.

Some minutes later, visualize the shaft descending from the neck to the chest; resting on the solar plexus — in other words, in the heart area. Here it forms a third sphere of bright light, extending from the front to the back of the chest, again the size of a salad plate. Maintain the keen visualization — or better yet, sense-feel it. The result is unmistakable.

It is here that we can see where some of the earlier exercises are yielding high dividends by making it easier to develop sensory awareness and feeling these whirling spheres.

Instead of the customary Hebrew name, which is very long and cumbersome, a Gnostic divine name will be used. It is shorter, vibrates extremely well and is much easier to use. This name is: IAO — which is pronounced: ee-ah-oh. Repeat the vibration of the name as often as may be required to help the mind to stay concentrated on the center. If necessary, a little dab of HEET on the middle of the breast-bone will produce enough skin sensation to help you become conscious of the area to be activated.

In about five minutes, visualize the shaft of light descending from the chest to the pelvic area, where a fourth sphere of light is formed in your imagination. Vibrate the name SHAD-DAI EL CHAI — shah-dye-ail-Cheye. (The Hebrew 'ch' is guttural as in the Scotch word for lake "loch".) Visualize and feel intense activity in this pelvic area, until the entire centre feels alive and pulsating with energy.

Finally, see the shaft of light descend from the pelvis to the feet, forming a fifth sphere of light. The name to be used here is ADONAI ha-ARETZ, pronounced: Ah-doh-nyehah-ah-retz. Vibrate the divine name often enough until it is felt in the lower extremities, stirring the sphere of light into vigorous activity. Feel it whirling and vibrating as a brilliant sphere of light-energy. Keep the mind concentrated on it for at least five minutes also.

A vast amount of spiritual energy has thus been stirred up and thrown into the organism. It now remains to circulate this energy throughout the entire system.

Go back in the imagination, to the top of the head and *will* that with the exhalation of the breath, the light-energy begins to stream down the length of the left side of the body to the feet. As you inhale, imagine this spiritual energy ascending the right side to the head center. Visualize this activity as a swiftly moving band of energy, extending out some distance from the body. Do this several times until some clear awareness of the movement has been achieved.

Then a similar imaginative gesture is to be followed with the energy flowing down the front of the body to the feet on exhalation, and ascending from the feet to the head at the back, on inhalation. This too should be imagined and felt occurring several times until the realization of movement is clear.

This sets up bands of energy circulating within and around the body forming a broad electro-magnetic field or aura of white light. The field is not yet complete, however, requiring but another gesture to round it out.

Return in the imagination to the foot center, and imagine that the Middle Pillar reaching up to the head center, is like a hollow pipe. On the inhalation of breath, suction is set up drawing the energy from the foot center up the hollow pipe, and on the exhalation it jets forth above the head center falling on all sides like a fountain. The energy sprays around the outer margins of the field, falling like a shower of scintillae to the feet, where it is once again gathered into the foot center. Upon inhalation, it is again drawn up into the Middle Pillar to be sprayed over the head upon exhalation. This process should be frequently repeated untl the result is a clear realization of a brilliant, vibrating field in which the student is enclosed and by which he is wholly permeated.

At this point, he should embark upon a meditation that he is enclosed in the Light of the Spirit and thereby is at one with the One Life which pulses through the universe and which unifies all beings and all things. If it will aid him to achieve the requisite degree of exaltation, he may recite something inspirational such as a passage from Crowley's *The World Tragedy:*

> Hear then! By Abrasax! The bar
> of the unshifting star
> Is broken — IO! Asar!
> My spirit is wrapt in the wind of light;
> It is whirled away on the wings of night,
> Sable-plumed are the wonderful wings,
> But the silver of moonlight subtly springs
> Into the feathers that flash with the pace
> Of our flight to the violate bounds of space.
> Time is dropt like a stone from the stars:
> Space is a chaos of broken bars:
> Being is merged in a furious flood
> That rages and hisses and foams in the blood.
> See! I am dead! I am passed, I am passed
> Out of the sensible world at last.

I am not. Yet I am, as I never was,
A drop in the sphere of molten glass
Whose radiance changes and shifts and drapes
The infinite soul in finite shapes.
There is light, there is life, there is love,
There is sense
Beyond speech, beyond song, beyond evidence.
There is wonder intense, a miraculous sun,
As the many are molten and mixed into one
With the heat of its passion; the one hath invaded
The heights of its soul, and its laughter is braided
With comets whose plumes are the galaxies
Like winds on the night's inaccessible seas.....

There may be another meaningful prayer or some other form of devotion that will prove exceedingly valuable to him. The exaltation of his mind to the highest peak of enlightenment, becomes possible at this particular juncture, depending on how intensely he has worked in formulating the divine white light of the spirit and how moved he has been by the contemplation of this paean of divine praise.

To close the exercise, he should give thanks for the experience and gradually withdraw the white sphere into himself, so that the field coincides with his own body. He should take a deep breath and tighten all his muscles to terminate the state and then stretch vigorously before getting up and going about his business.

In closing and giving thanks, the following could be used:

Unto thee, sole Wise, sole Eternal and Sole Merciful One be the praise and the glory forever, who has permitted me, who now standeth humbly before Thee, to enter thus far into the sanctuary of thy mystery. Not unto me, but unto Thy name be the glory. Let the influence of thy divine ones descend upon my head and teach me the value of self-sacrifice, so that I shrink not in the hour of trial. But that thus my name may be written upon high and my Genius stand in the presence of the holy Ones in that hour when the Son of Man is invoked before the

Lord of Spirits and his name in the presence of the Ancient of Days. Amen.

This Middle Pillar technique is another of those exercises which may take far more than a single month to master. In any event, the student may discover that he wishes to use it more or less intermittently or continuously throughout the entire course of his life. It has infinite possibilities which only persistent practice will indicate.

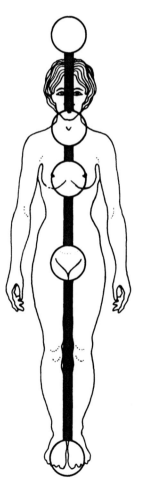

The Middle Pillar

STEP IX
SYMBOL OF DEVOTION

IT IS AXIOMATIC THAT ANY strongly felt emotion will produce as a by-product a mental concentration of an intense kind. For example, if some event has occurred to produce a fearful reaction, it may seem almost impossible to some people to switch the mind over to another topic. One becomes consumed, as it were, with the fear, concentrated wholly upon it to the exclusion of all else, breathing and living this emotion, no matter how much one might like to think of something else. This is why, in some of the psychoneuroses, the patient appears to be concerned wholly with his pathological feelings and despite prodding and reassurance cannot really turn his mind in another direction. *The emotion induces concentration.*

A man or woman in the early stages of being in love neglects all other preoccupations but his beloved. Morning, noon and night — eating, resting or waking, he is concerned solely with his emotions and his beloved. Some people speak of this kind of love as being mad or insane. It may well appear to be so, since the preoccupation or concentration is so all-consuming, but as I am trying to indicate here, any powerful emotion produces this same end-result.

Since we are attempting by a series of widely differing devices to produce a state of concentration, it behooves us to become aware of the dynamic effect of emotion on the organism. Everyone has had this experience at some time or another in his life and so is on speaking terms with what is being discussed here. What we have to do, therefore, is to devise some method of awakening enough feeling or of stimulating a sufficiently powerful emotion which can be consciously and deliberately employed as a tool to be used for turning the mind wholly to one topic. It is fervor and profound conviction that are required here as the productive and creative agency.

So let us cast around for something that will tend to awaken a profoundly moving reaction. Search your memory. What moves you emotionally? A sentence from the Bible — from one of the Psalms or the Epistles? A crucifix or some other religious symbol? A poem? Or a memory of an exciting love affair of years gone by — or even proceeding today?

Whatever it is, think upon it. Examine it closely and carefully. Picture it vividly. Even go as far as to draw or paint or to reproduce in some other way — something that will serve as a symbol of that which excites the emotion, a symbol which we can now call the beloved. And by only a slight effort, a very mild stretch of the imagination, this symbol of the beloved can be extended to include or to become the goal of all the preceding work itself, which we call the Great Work. This is nothing more or less than the total transformation of man from a sense-oriented creature to one who is conscious of his being a vehicle of the One Universal Life, a human being who is illuminated by the gnosis, the knowledge that God exists within as well as without him. *"For I have found Thee in the Me and the Thee. In the One and the Many have I found Thee, yea, I have found Thee."*

While formulating the symbol of the goal of one's devotion, you can either render it objectively as in a drawing or painting of some object which can be regarded as sacred, or maintain it abstractly as a symbol within the mind itself without expressing it concretely at all. Thus it can be an idea, or a memory of a person who was beloved, or a verse from a poem or a sacred scripture. For example, I have often used the following:

> *The prophet cried against the mountain: come thou hither that I may speak with Thee!*

The mountain stirred not. Therefore went the
prophet unto the mountain, and spake unto it.
But the feet of the prophet were weary and the
mountain heard not his voice.
But I have called unto Thee, and I have journeyed
unto Thee, and it availed me not.
I waited patiently and thou wast with me from
the beginning. This now I know,
O my beloved, and we are stretched
at our ease among the vines.
But these Thy prophets; they must cry aloud and
scourge themselves; they must cross trackless
wastes and unfathomed oceans; to await Thee is
the end, not the beginning.

There is a painting by Salvador Dali of a crucifixion which also is most meaningful to me. This Dali painting takes the point of view of some heavenly seer above looking down on the crucifixion below — from the trancendental point of view, as it were. It is extremely effective, and there have been occasions when I have employed it as a symbol to awaken devotion.

Throughout the years I have also come to use a far more abstract symbol, the Hebrew letter *Shin* ש. It has, Qabalistically, the numerical value of 300 — which also happens to be the same value for a Hebrew phrase meaning *The Spirit of the Living God.* So that this one letter-symbol embodies for me a vast series of intellectual ideas and aspirations. It has thus developed as a symbol of the highest aspirations and as a fiery triple-tongued flame of light, I frequently have visualized it overshadowing me.

But whatever it is, lavish attention upon the symbol until it becomes so powerful a force that merely upon seeing it or by thinking about it, is enough to awaken an intense feeling of ardor and devotion. Once this point has been reached, then wherever one goes, the symbol goes, and devotion awakens spontaneously and grows. Waking or sleeping, eating or drinking, shaving or dressing, combing one's hair or applying cosmetics, it remains in the background of one's mind to represent the beloved upon which one is concentrated. With this development, it becomes symbolic to consecrate one's every activity to the service of the beloved. Each act is done for the beloved, regardless of what it is and no matter how ordinary or commonplace it may seem. It leads ultimately to the dedication of one's life to God, to render holy every hitherto worthless or minute deed and perfunctory act. Life becomes consecrated — and all one's energies become automatically concentrated in one continuous act of devotion to the beloved — to God, or whatever one chooses to call the One Universal and Eternal Life that courses through each one of us, uniting us in a higher synthesis that is at the same time the multiplicity of division.

Step X
PRACTICE OF THE
PRESENCE OF GOD

I WOULD LIKE YOU TO REVIEW some of the exercises you have done much earlier in this course. Review especially the exercise of watching the body and all its sensations without interfering and also the one of observing the activity of the mind without in the least attempting to stop the flow of thoughts and memories. Spend a couple of days actively reviewing the method and practice so that the skill previously acquired becomes reactivated. In other words, reinforce the original conditioned reflex by renewed exercise.

What I am asking you to do now after this review is to consider the obvious fact that the skin all over the body is perforated by millions of minute holes which we call *pores*. Every organ in the body, being composed of cells of different types and sizes, similarly is perforated by countless intercellular spaces, interstices of minute size. In other words, by a contemplation of this anatomical fact — which can be demonstrated by examining the surface of any portion of the skin, anywhere, with a high-powered magnifying glass — the student will begin to realize that the concept of physical solidity and impermeability is merely a convenient concept — but not necessarily an accurate one.

The student should lie down on a couch on his back, in the formal relaxation position. Later, when considerable skill has been achieved, he will not need to recline in this or any other special way. Relaxation will occur so immediately that it can be induced anywhere, at any time, merely by willing it to occur. But for the initial purpose of acquiring mastery of the technique he should recline, with closed eyes, in order to block out all sensory impressions from the external world. Lying down, then, relaxed, imagine the skin on the cheeks of the face, feeling that the pores in the skin are stretched wide open — large yawning precipices and lacunae on the face. A few seconds work will usually suffice — especially if he has previously followed the former exercises month by month and acquired some facility in concentrating the mind and making it follow the will.

Extend this notion then to the skin on the forehead, nose and entire face. Include also, piecemeal, the scalp and the back of the head. Contemplate, in each area, that no longer is the skin impermeable and non-porous, but that it is composed of more holes than tissue. In fact, the picture of a woman's hairnet (even though these are rarely seen nowadays) will perfectly convey the idea to be grasped.

In much the same way, the entire body should be visualized, following the surface of the skin downwards from the head, neck, shoulders and arms, thorax, pelvis and abdomen, thighs, legs and feet. He should consider every part, coming to realize that the membrane which surrounds every organ of the body, holding it together as a limiting membrane, has lost its density and impermeability and is actually a series of holes loosely knit together by a net-like tissue. Reaching the toes and soles of the feet, he should pause temporarily to acquire the full sensation of the stretching of the pores — a completely unmistakable sensation.

This sensation, once acquired — and no further work on this exercise should be continued until it is acquired — now let him return to reflection of the head once more. But this time, his imagination will extend interiorly rather than externally. He should try to consider the brain, not as in the preliminary relaxation technique with a view to vascularising its neural tissue, but in order to arrive at the feeling that it too has become full of holes. The student should attempt to acquire the sensation that the interstices between the brain cells are becoming greater, and that the brain is, in a word, becoming sponge-like. If he can first examine a real sponge, he will have succeeded in realizing what I am attempting to describe by feeling that the substance of the brain is similarly constructed. This may take some little time, but once obtained it can be induced again with the greatest of ease.

This sponge feeling should now be applied to every organ of the body, one after the other. Deal with the head area first of all. Feel, in turn, that the brain, the eyes, the nose, the ears, all the viscera of the head, are sponge-like, replacing the solid tissue. Even the bony covering of the head, the skull, when examined under a microscope or with large magnification is seen to be full of holes. Use this fact. Then continue with the neck, imagining that the neck vertebrae of the spine, the neck muscles and flesh, larynx, esophagus and other glands — in fact, visualizing that the whole neck has become like a number of sponges, nothing but holes bound together by a membrane. Apply a similar technique to the shoulder and arms. Visualize that a bone, as well as muscles and ligaments and tendons, respond to exactly the same image. The thorax with its soft organs of lungs, heart, large blood-vessels, etc. likewise comprise a large sponge. In fact, the lungs and liver, and many another organ, when examined microscopically, do look very much like spongy tissue. The abdomen, pelvis, thigh and legs then disappear save as they appear to the imagination, or are felt, as masses of holes bound into an integrated whole.

It is important that this realization be obtained fully before he continues. It is not very difficult really, and most people can obtain it within a very short period of time. Any student who has persevered with this course of training up to this point should experience no difficulty at all. The physical sensations attending this sponge-realization are distinctive and cannot be mistaken for any other bodily reaction.

As an aside, the student should try to remember the dictum of Berkeleyan philosophy, that sensation tells us not immediately of material objects, but only of divine ideas retained in the universal mind of God — this will enable him to transcend the plane of mere technique. If this presents difficulties, at least let him realize that sensations are cerebral activities — that without the brain there could be no knowledge of sensation; that, in effect, sensations are psychological processes. We are at all times dealing with mind and its activities — and with nothing else.

If the body is thus full of perforations, the student should consider this fact. Since the atmosphere encloses him and surrounds him at all times, the now-absolutely-permeable body offers no impediment whatsoever to the entrance of air from any quarter. In fact, so far from resisting the flow of air through his body, he knows that the atmosphere must literally rush and course through these myriads of holes which he now feels his body to be. As he reclines on the couch, fully relaxed, let him now imagine that the surrounding air pours through his body, pushing downwards from the ceiling. He may combine this with the rhythms of his breathing, as already described earlier.

As he breathes in, let him realize that the air saturates the sponge that he is, pouring into him from above, from head to toe. With the exhalation of breath, the air leaves his porous body, making its exit all the way along the back of his head, the back of his trunk, thighs, and legs. Continue this notion for some several seconds until the feeling of the permeability of the body to the surrounding air grows. Let the student vary the exercise, first by imagining that he breathes in through the pores in the soles of his feet, the air rushing vigorously along the whole course of his body, and exhaling through the crown of his head and vice-versa. Then that the atmosphere rises up from below him, passing out through him in front to rise to the ceiling above.

These are simply a series of imaginative concepts which have the effect of furthering the relaxation of the body and mind begun in earlier months, and at the same time preparing the trained mind to consider new spiritual truths. The spiritual fact to be considered is the primordial relationship existing between air and spirit. In all primitive languages, the word for air is the same as that for spirit and mind. Both are life and the carriers of life. Without air there can be no manifestation of life.

Let the student therefore begin to consider psychologically the notion that this air rushing through his body so completely open to its influx, and offering no impediment or barrier — this air is the Divine Spirit. It is the universal life which animates all created things. This all-pervasive Air is the immanent God who, so all the metaphysical systems teach, is an omnipresent, infinite, omnipotent principle. Spirit is everywhere at all times, and there is no part of space which is exempt from its presence. God is all-powerful; we cannot conceive of any competing or opposing force. Nor can we conceive that He should have any limitations of any kind that our minds can conceive of. He is divine wisdom and truth and all our knowledge and learning is but an infinitesimal fragment of the omniscience of the Universal Spirit. He, likewise, is all-love; an all-embracing love that is so fine and broad and intense that those who touch that love in their consciousness, rave of the ineffable ecstasy and bliss that came in their realization. All these qualities belong to God, and these are the characteristics that the student should contemplate as he begins to consider the relationship of Spirit with air — the air that rushes through his body and mind.

By imagining the air to saturate the completely porous and permeable body, we are in reality, arriving at a high consciousness of the ever-presence and power of God. God pervades every minute cell of the body. No atom, no minute particle anywhere in this body can possibly be free of the power and substance and love that God is. All the previous knowledge and practical mystical experience that the student has acquired may now be thrown with the utmost intensity and concentration into this meditation — for such it is — with the complete assurance and knowledge that he has achieved success. He has already gained confidence in the efficacy of his own efforts by having applied himself to the techniques already described and which he has assiduously practiced.

This Practice of the Presence of God is only an extension of earlier work. A true realization of his identity with God's infinite spirit may thus be divined, in such a way that no violence is done either to body or to mind. All parts of man are fulfilled, justified without unnatural denial or negligence, hence the realization obtained of God must be full and complete — a perfect and harmonious indentification with divine power and life and love.

Step XI
UNITY — ALL IS GOD

I who *made* the Universe *am* the Universe: and abide its separate Lord.
Song Celestial

Now that, through the pursuit of this series of psycho-spiritual disciplines, some degree of God-realization has been achieved (though never let it be forgotten for one second that this is but a beginning and a beginning only) the student is faced by a most important decision. He is obliged to eradicate every vestige of duality from his thinking. Residues will cling to his mind, in very subtle ways. There is no God *and* the World — there is not God and himself. There is *only* God. All is God. Every trivial action is God-directed. Every single object in his environment is God-endowed. Even the ego — though that seems to be the major obstacle to be gotten rid of — is God-determined.

Yet he is a man or woman living for the moment in what appears to be a material world. He has to accept the world of appearances, the phenomenal world, exactly as it is. There, in that phenomenal world, heat burns, cold freezes, water is wet, concrete is hard and his body needs nutrition of every kind. Although each and everyone of these phenomena are divine phenomena — and in their constant change are nonetheless representative of the ceaseless activity of the unchanging, omnipotent body of God — yet he must learn to keep all these diverse phenomena in their own place. Because he realizes his essential identity with the Life in all things howsoever diverse, yet he has to realize as well that these phenomena have their distinct laws which must be respected and obeyed.

While he may fly with the speed of light on other levels and walk through apparently solid walls and know full well the illusoriness of time, yet here and now he must live by the clock and travel by car or train or plane in order to go where he will. And he will find it more circumspect and certainly easier to walk through a door rather than to try to squeeze himself through the molecular structure of a wall. Each plane has its own laws; these too are God. And God in all His phases and activities is God.

What then shall he do when it is necessary for him, as a man in the phenomenal world, to work His Will, to achieve other of his goals? What if, in all humility, he realizes that his job, whatever that may be, depletes his energies so that no longer is there satisfaction to be obtained from it? He needs a vacation. Where shall he go? And how shall it be financed?

His car is now a worn-out old jalopy. It becomes expensive to run and repair, is a menace on the highway and demands far too much of his attention in order to be handled well. How shall he get another?

He is surrounded by people who do not know that they are God-enlightened. he knows and feels they are; this knowledge is a part of his own mystical realization. They are hysterical, anxious, compulsive, disturbed by one event or problem after another, are sick and lame and halt. All this because they know not what or who they truly are.

How shall we presume to make them aware of their true nature without invading their precious privacy?

In other words, though he knows his own personal relationship to God, he must consider what practical engines are to be used to fulfill his Will. He must consider those methods whereby his needs are to be met that the divine purpose may be fulfilled.

There are many ways, of course, to do this. One of these is the method described in a little book I wrote some years ago, *The Art of True Healing*. It is a method of mobilizing the spiritual power of the cosmos through the agency of Will, color, imagination and sound in order to achieve that which is required. It is an extension of the Middle Pillar where divine energy is concentrated and directed for specific use. It does not need to be other than mentioned here; it has great merit and is far from difficult to use. (It is now one essay in a book entitled *Foundations of Practical Magic*, Aquarian Press, England 1979.)

There is another approach which is possible only to that student who has persevered with his own disciplines so that he has become an avenue through which the Divine Will may operate. Its outstanding merit is that it is simple and direct. It is not dissimilar to the classical religious one of accepting Jesus as one's personal Lord and Savior, and turning one's life over to Him. This approach has it that we are eager to find Him when we come to realize that there is no source of power in ourselves, that we are wholly dependent on Him. We become eager to connect up with this Source of Life and Power when we know that it makes wisdom, power and love available for us. It is "the strait gate," "the narrow way," and "few there be that find it." This is the traditional evangelistic Christian way.

In this work, instead of using the traditional and formalistic terms of the Christ consciousness, we fall back on the mystico-magical tradition to use the term "The Holy Guardian Angel" as the term for our own Higher Self. He is an angel, mighty and powerful and is our own personal link with the universal God, and so it is to Him that we submit ourselves for the fulfillment of His Will, which at the same time and paradoxically, is our will.

We have to learn experientially, the wisdom and meaning of those beautiful verses in the second chapter of *The Light on the Path*, where Mabel Collins wrote:

1. Stand aside in the coming battle, and though thou fightest be not thou the warrior.

2. Look for the Warrior and let him fight in thee.

3. Take his orders for battle and obey them.

4. Obey him not as though he were a general, but as though he were thyself, and his spoken words were the utterance of thy secret desires; for he is thyself, yet infinitely wiser and stronger than thyself. Look for him, else in the fever and hurry of the fight thou mayest pass him; and he will not know thee unless thou knowest him.

If thy cry reach his listening ear then will he fight in thee and fill the dull void within. And if this is so, then canst thou go through the fight cool and unwearied, standing aside and letting him battle for thee. Then it will be impossible for thee to strike one blow amiss. But if thou look not for him, if thou pass him by, then there is no safeguard for thee. Thy brain will reel, thy heart grow uncertain, and in the dust of the battlefield thy sight and senses will fail, and thou will not know thy friends from thy enemies.

"He is thyself, yet thou art but finite and liable to error. He is eternal and is sure. He is eternal truth. When once he has entered thee and become thy Warrior, he will never utterly desert thee, and at the day of the great peace he will become one with thee."

We cannot make a vital contact with our Angel by goodness or obedience — these latter characteristics merely follow when we have found Him. Then goodness and obedience and the other socalled virtues take on another meaning altogether, far removed from that understood in the bourgeois or conventional morality.

Nor may we find him because of our good deeds. At best, our good deeds are only the evidence that we have found him. Then we may find that instead of good they are selfish — but dedicated to the Self that is the Angel. Nor do we find Him by a belief in any religious, metaphysical or occult doctrine. At best these are intellectual constructs for the expansion of our minds but later come to have profound meaning as useful constructs only after we have found Him.

If we are willing to persevere, to be patient, and to work at self-discipline, to aspire and to invoke often, the Angel will enable us to do all of this. For every step we make in His direction, he will take two. *Thou wast long seeking Me; thou didst run forward so fast that I was unable to come up with thee. O thou darling fool! What bitterness thou didst crown thy days withal. Now I am with thee; I will never leave thy being.*

We do not have to do violence to ourselves to force ourselves to believe in Him; there is no need for force. We do not have to will ourselves to believe. We need only to be willing, to make the necessary set of gestures, sincerely and honestly — and then *work and invoke often!*

It entails trusting the Holy Guardian Angel with all areas of our lives. In this we must face our egotism to realize that of ourselves we can do nothing, and what we are able to do can only result in futility and frustration. It means trusting the Angel to renew our character; we cannot do it ourselves. We turn over to Him the entire psyche, with all its conscious and unconscious problems and complexes which we have become acquainted with through the agency of the former exercises — and perhaps through some psychotherapeutic work. But we leave it to Him to clean out the filth from the stables — when it ceases to be filth. Only He can do it; of ourselves we are impotent.

It means allowing Him to dictate all our activities and keeping our hands and minds from meddling with His work, reserving them only as tools which He can use as He sees fit for our betterment and progress. We must not interfere with what He has to do.

It means trusting Him as to our health and financial security. This does not mean that we become careless of our nutritional intake, our clothes or personal hygiene or that we drive the automobile with eyes closed. But it does mean that we stop worrying about what is going to become of us. We do the very best we can in any situation, knowing that He is guiding and guarding us — and letting Him worry about us.

It means laying aside all our petty ambitions and objectives and permitting Him to plan our life for us. It may not result in the fulfillment of every ambition and objective, but we learn to rely solely upon Him, knowing that we will be guided constantly and continuously whether we are aware of it or not.

It means putting away all our nice little occult philosophies and systems where everything is put into a neat cubbyhole and neatly compartmentalized and letting Him lead us to the Truth. It is the joy of putting aside our human frailties, of allowing Him to sanctify us so that we fall not into the pit called *because* where we may perish with the dogs of reason.

In this, we find a new wisdom, a new joy, and a new illumined way of dealing with life. To the onlooker, who knows nothing of this inner transformation, very little difference in our behavior may be observed. To us however, it means that *not I live, but Jesus Christ liveth in me.* This is the magical way, of letting the Angel do His work among the living, of having placed oneself under the aegis of the Angel after having worked and prayed and invoked.

From now on, the responsibility for all one's life in all its phases is taken from our petty egos wth its limited vision and scope, and its wretched lust for results, and surrendered gladly to this higher agency which is *Oneself Made Perfect.*

It is then that he can sing the triumphant peroration to the ancient Ritual in which he glorifies his unity with the Angel in these dynamic terms:

> *I am He, the bornless Spirit, having sight in the feet, strong, and the immortal Fire.*
> *I am He, the Truth.*
> *I am He, who hate that evil should be wrought in the world.*
> *I am He, that lighteneth and thundereth.*
> *I am He, from whom is the shower of the Life of Earth.*
> *I am He, whose mouth ever flameth.*
> *I am He, the begetter and manifestor unto the Light.*
> *I am He, the Grace of the World.*
> *'The Heart Girt with a Serpent is my name.'*

STEP XII
INVOKE OFTEN!
INFLAME THYSELF WITH
PRAYER!

THE STUDENT WHO HAS persevered to this point, should by now find that his efforts are paying magnificent dividends. A number of results should have occurred — the least of them being an enormous expansion in the horizons of his consciousness. It could well be that, in addition, he is acquiring an awareness of divinity, his own divinity, as well as that of the immanent and transcendent God in whom we *live, move and have our being.* Through the practice of the presence of God he should be able to extend his awareness so vastly that wherever he is, and regardless of the apparent triviality of his activity, he knows that God goes with him. He rests in the bosom of the Eternal — and realizes the meaning of being *under the shadow of Thy wings.*

With this high achievement, he might feel tempted to relax in order to rest upon his laurels. And it may well be that for a period of time, he should do just that, as though to enjoy the rewards of his long and hard labor and permit himself to recoup his energies as though to prepare for the long climb ahead. But this accomplished, he has to gird up his loins and move forward, remembering the instruction of the Chaldean Oracles that one must *"invoke often"* and *"inflame himself with prayer"* according to The Book of Sacred Magic of Abra-Melin the Mage. There are higher goals to aspire towards and through the exaltation of prayer or invocation, he may, God willing, reach these goals, unitive and mystical.

Daily discipline is surely required. All spiritual teachers in some way recognize this and therefore recommend a daily period of prayer. "Every soul must take time daily for quiet and meditation," writes Emilie Cady in her *Lessons in Truth*. "In daily meditation lies the secret of power. No one can grow in either spiritual knowledge or power without it. Practice the Presence of God just as you would practice music. No one would ever dream of becoming a power in music except by spending some time daily alone with music. Daily meditation alone with God, seems in some way, to focus the divine presence within us and our consciousness."

There are many methods for achieving quiet and meditation. Some people, for example, will use any previously quoted prayer when they have achieved some familiarity with the quiet state created within. In fact, they use it to create for themselves the serenity and self-assurance they long for. It seems to possess the self-imposed and self-devised power of exalting them ecstatically to a consciousness of the omnipresence of God who, upon explicit invitation, as it were, will be able to act through the individual. He will, in this way, come to feel and realize his implicit relationship and necessitous reliance upon God.

For much the same purpose, Crowley's *Holy Books* likewise are used by many people. It is needless to indicate that the *Holy Books* breathe a warm atmosphere of adoration, of ecstatic praise of God. Probably the Psalms are the best examples of the poetic beauty of the Bible, indicating that the Psalmist knew God at first-hand, had ineffable experience of Him pulsing vibrantly in the heart's blood and in the loins, a living presence, strong, vital and passionate.

The metaphysical argument is that by dwelling upon a poem or statement or prayer uttered by a spiritually enlightened person, by a mind that knew God in intimate communion, the reader or listener with sympathetic understanding and devotion, will find his mind exalted to similar heights of spiritual discernment and realization. Like will speak unto like and the phenomenon of sympathetic vibration will awaken him to a realization of the divine consciousness within, in a holy and mystical experience.

Prayer does have the effect of stimulating the mind to function in an entirely new way. It creates, when successful, a revolution within the psychological apparatus, a turning around of the mind. It becomes ecstatically uplifted so as to function in a new way, to perceive new and more spiritual ideas, and experience a hitherto never before experienced life of divinity and high consciousness. The entire object of prayer is to exalt the mind to *an indissoluble unity with God.* It must lift the mind on the wings of ardent aspiration — thus the phrase "inflame thyself with prayer" — in an unrestrained flight of love to a sense of kinship and unity with the whole of life.

There must be this ardor. An attitude of cold objectivity and lack of feeling during prayer is, so far as my understanding goes, quite impossible. I cannot conceive how the student who has pondered over a classical invocation and understood it to the extent of employing it as his personal means of exaltation, can refrain from being strongly moved emotionally. A prayer, to be successful, should have the effect of bringing about an inner crisis. More often than not, as the student proceeds, he will be bathed in a deluge of tears — tears not of sorrow, nor even tears of joy, but tears which are the sign and symbol of submission to and union with, the Source of All Life.

An ecstasy may result, a thoroughgoing standing out of the mind itself and all its concerns with the body and its problems, from neurosis and inner turmoils. It should raise the individual above all temporal and personal matters so as to realize that the heresy of separation is ended for all time. He and God are one!

The whole secret of prayer lies in this direction. *Invoke often. Inflame thyself with prayer.* It aims at moving the individual in ecstasy to transcend himself. In short, prayer consists of a complex of psychological and spiritual gestures — all of which should prove relatively easy, after the prolonged discipline engaged in for the past several months or more — designed to enable us to recover our true identity, which is God.

I would like to give two prayers or invocations — they are equivalent terms — which I have found of infinite value in my personal spiritual life. It is my hope that each student may find them equally rich and inspirational.

The first one should be used in the morning — for it is my suggestion that at least two or three periods be set apart in the day, periods of up to an hour apiece, to be opened up by a swift relaxing process to prepare for the use of the prayer. Both should be memorized thoroughly, so that there is no stumbling or need for reflection over the next phrase, and so that the sole effort be reserved for developing that fever pitch which is the sole requirement for success:

I am the Resurrection and the Life. Whosoever believeth on me, though he were dead, yet shall he live; and whosoever liveth and believeth on me, the same shall never die. I am the First and I am the Last. I am He that liveth and was dead — and behold! I am alive forever more, and hold the keys of hell and of death.

For I know that my Redeemer liveth and that he shall stand at the latter day upon the earth. I am the Way, the Truth and the Life. No man cometh unto the Father save by me.

I am the Purified. I have passed through the gates of darkness unto light. I have fought upon earth for good. I have finished my work and entered into the invisible.

I am the Preparer of the Pathway, the Rescuer unto the Light. I am the Reconciler with the Ineffable, the Dweller of the Invisible. Let the White Brilliance of the Divine Spirit descend.

Daily use of this ritual-prayer, with as much ardor as can be mustered, will gradually bring about the unitive state which is enlightenment.

The evening period for prayer should last the same length of time and should be felt keenly and vividly until literally every hair of one's body stands on end during its utterance. I strongly recommend the following traditional prayer after the student has completed the preliminary relaxation techniques.

From Thy hand, O Lord, cometh all good. The characters of nature with Thy fingers has Thou traced, but none can read them unless he hast been taught in Thy school. Therefore, even as servants look unto the hands of their masters, and handmaidens unto their mistresses, even so do our eyes look unto Thee, for Thou alone art our help. O Lord our God, who should not extol Thee?

All is from Thee, All belongeth unto Thee. Either Thy love or Thy anger, all must again re-enter. Nothing canst Thou lose, for all must tend unto Thy honour and majesty. Thou art Lord alone, and there is none beside Thee. Thou doest what Thou wilt with Thy mighty arm, and none can escape from Thee.

Who should not praise Thee, then, O Lord of the Universe, unto whom there is none like? Whose dwelling is in heaven, and in every virtuous and God-fearing heart. O God, Thou vast One, Thou art in all things. O Nature, Thou Self from Nothing — for what else can I call Thee? In myself I am nothing. In Thee I am Self, and exist in Thy Selfhood from eternity. Live Thou in me, and bring me unto That self which is in Thee.

EPILOGUE

This final chapter could just as well have been placed at the beginning of this book. But then the student would have had to accept the doctrine of the *Inner Warrior* on faith. And for some people today, faith is unknown or difficult to come by. In any event, in the mystico-magical technique described, faith in that sense of the word, is not called for.

The emphasis throughout has been on a series of techniques, meditations and disciplines which, first of all, produce their own results. The major one however, is an enormous increase in sensitivity and self-awareness which provides the sure knowledge that there are aspects and phases of our being which have yet to be explored and known. When this certain knowledge has been acquired, then the submission by faith to the *Inner Warrior, The Holy Guardian Angel,* is a logical and spiritual necessity. It may humble our minds and egos, but it will not outrage our sense of rightness to have faith in something of which we have no direct knowledge or perception. *Living by faith in the Angel* can only be used, as a technique of the spiritual life, when the preceding disciplines have been practiced, accepted and employed. Thus its placement at the end of the book.

Moreover, we must not fall into the booby trap of believing that henceforward, life will present us with no problems, that all will be made easy. This is never so. As long as we live on this earth, there will be problems and difficulties. But though these exist, and though we may make many mistakes, nonetheless, by adhering to our vision of the *Holy Guardian Angel* or *Inner Warrior,* each difficulty and mistake becomes transformed into a means whereby we grow in spiritual stature. The rough edges of our being become rounded and polished, the flaws in our makeup become character, and we grow more akin to the heart's desire and become absorbed in the holy nature of the Angel who is the Self.

RECOMMENDED READING

This *One Year Manual* is essentially a practical course for personal development. Very little attention has been given to theory or philosophy. In the event the interested student wishes to pursue further the intellectual study of the various practices comprising this program, the following books are recommended.

The Way of a Pilgrim. Translated by R.M. French (Seabury Press, New York, 1968).
The Perrenial Philosophy. Aldous Huxley (Harper, N.Y., 1944).
Teachings of the Mystics. W.T. Stace (Mentor Books).
The Christian's Secret of a Happy Life. Hannah Whitall Smith (Fleming H. Revell Co. N.Y. 1941)
Mysticism. Evelyn Underhill (Meridian Books, N.Y. 1955)
The Candle of Vision. A.E. (Macmillans, London, 1919)
Varieties of Religious Experience. William James. (Mentor Books)
Science of Breath. Yogi Ramacharaka (Yogi Publication Society, Chicago, 1904)
Ramakrishna and His Disciples. Christopher Isherwood. (Simon & Schuster, N.Y. 1959)
Loaves & Fishes. Hereward Carrington (Scribners, N.Y. 1935)
Lessons in Truth. Emilie Cady. (Unity, Kansas 1939)
The Christos. Vitvan (School of the Natural Order, Baker, Nev. 1951)